JAZZ GUITAR

sight-reading

MW01131553

Contents

Musical Symbols 2

A Few Words About Sight-Reading 3

The "Jazz" Feel 3

Using a Metronome 3

Using the CD 3

Section 1: Blues Etudes 4

About Jazz Rhythms 12

Section 2: Rhythm Studies 14

Section 3: Etudes Based on Jazz Standards 20

Section 4: Duets 32

Bio

Guitarist/composer Adam Levy is a native of Los Angeles, where he attended the Dick Grove School of Music and studied with Ted Greene. He spent the early 1990s making a name for himself in San Francisco, teaching at the Blue Bear School of Music and performing with some of the Bay Area's most interesting groups. This ultimately led to touring and performing with Tracy Chapman, who featured Levy on her Grammy Award-winning song "Give Me One Reason." Respected as a teacher as well as a performer, Levy is a regular faculty member at the National Guitar Summer Workshop and has contributed several instructional articles to *Guitar Player* Magazine. He presently lives in New York City.

Introduction

The purpose of this book is to provide jazz-oriented sight-reading material for guitarists at an intermediate level. The exercises are written using common jazz-style phrases and are intended to be played with a "jazz" or "swing" feel.

The music is presented in four sections. The first section is a series of blues etudes intended to help you familiarize yourself with different positions on the guitar. The second section consists of jazz rhythm studies. The third section is a series of etudes in the style of famous jazz tunes, such as *All the Things You Are* and *Stella by Starlight*. The final section is a series of duets; some are in the style of popular jazz standards and some are my own original compositions.

I hope you enjoy the music. Many books on the subject of reading are full of black dots, but don't have much to offer in the way of real music. It was my goal in writing this book to provide students with music that is fun to play, as well as challenging.

One final note: our goal in sight-reading is to be able to play a piece of music with little or no preparation. If you make mistakes, try playing at a slower tempo, but do not stop in the middle to practice a difficult passage. Finish playing the piece. Our motto is "forward ever, backward

Best of luck.

Cover photos: Jeff Oshiro

Musical Symbols used in this book.

 Go back to the beginning and play again.

 Go back to the repeat sign and play again.

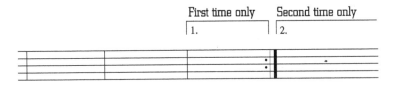 Play 1st ending first time, repeat to the beginning, then skip 1st ending and play 2nd ending.

D. C. al Fine   Go back to the beginning and end at *Fine.*

D. C. al Coda   Go back to the beginning and play to the coda sign (⊕), then skip to the *Coda* to end the piece.

Other Musical Symbols you are likely to see in music you will play.

D. S. al Fine   Go back to the sign (𝄋) and end at *Fine.*

D. S. al Coda   Go back to the sign (𝄋) and play to the coda sign (⊕), then skip to the *Coda* to end the piece.

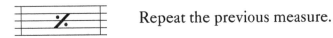 Repeat the previous measure.

 Repeat the previous two measures.

A Few Words About Sight-Reading

When students ask me what they should do to develop their reading skills, my answer is always the same: *Read*. Like any other area of skill, there aren't too many "secrets," just real practice. That being said, I do want to mention a few things that will help you to get the most out of this book and any other reading material.

The first rule is to look ahead. Just as when you're driving a car, you wouldn't dare to think of only looking at the ten feet of asphalt you happen to be on at the moment. You look out in front of you, as far as you can see, in order to be prepared for any obstacles that may be coming your way.

You can also improve your reading skills by learning to memorize. Try this: Look at the first measure of a piece of music and then look away or close your eyes and play what you can remember. With practice, you can memorize two, four, eight or more measures. This is a skill that you must develop in order to maximize your reading ability. It will allow you to look even farther ahead in the music and it will allow you to look at other people—the audience, the other musicians, the conductor—while you are playing.

Sometimes you can use "games" to help keep your practice time fun and interesting. One game is to take a piece of music and play every other measure (play the first measure, then jump to the third measure, then the fifth, etc.). This forces you to use your peripheral vision and look even farther ahead. Get creative—read every other measure, then try every third or fourth measure. You could even try reading down the page vertically. In other words, play the first measure of the first staff, then the first measure of the second staff, etc. When you get to the bottom you can go back to the top and read the down the second measure of each staff, then the third measure of each staff, and so on.

Perhaps the most important thing to keep in mind when practicing sight-reading is to not stop. If you hit a wrong note, just keep going. This will take a lot of concentration, as you will probably be tempted to stop and fix your mistakes. That's fine when you're working on a piece of music for a performance, but when you're practicing

reading you must not stop. This may mean playing at a slower tempo until your ability to sight-read improves.

Remember, the best way to become a better reader is to read. So, what are you waiting for? Dust off your music stand and your metronome, and let's go for it.

The "Jazz" Feel

Almost all of the music in this book is intended to be played with a "jazz" feel. This means that two consecutive eighth notes should sound more like the first and third notes of an eighth-note triplet. This gives the music a "swing" feel. The exceptions to this are the duets "Dolphins on Green Street," "Hymn-like" and "Kenny D." These should be played as written, with even eighth notes or "straight eighths."

Using a Metronome

When practicing reading, it's important to use a metronome to help you to keep a steady tempo. This is particularly important in sight-reading.

Many jazz players like to practice with their metronome clicking only the off-beats. In other words, if you're practicing a piece of music at 100 beats per minute, set your metronome to 50 beats per minute and think of the clicks as "2" and "4" Try practicing something simple, like a scale. After that becomes comfortable, try playing some of the rhythm studies in this book.

Using the CD

A CD is available demonstrating all the music in this book. The track numbers on the CD correspond with the track numbers listed throughout the book. For the Etudes Based on Jazz Standards section, the guitar part can be tuned out by using the balance control, enabling you to play along with the rhythm section. For the Duets section, you can tune out either guitar part allowing you to play either part with the CD. Be sure you have practiced the music before listening to the demonstrations on the CD.

Introduction and Tuning Track 1

4

Section #1: Blues Etudes

These etudes were written to help you get familiar with different positions on the guitar. Playing "in position" means keeping your fretting hand in one specific place on the neck, and using only one finger per fret. If you are in "third position," use your first finger for notes in the third fret, your second finger for notes in the fourth fret, your third finger for notes in the fifth fret and your fourth finger for notes in the sixth fret. You can also use your first finger to stretch to the second fret and

your fourth finger can stretch to the seventh fret.

Some of the etudes are in positions that may seem awkward. If an etude seems particularly difficult, try a slower tempo. If it's still too hard, try a higher or lower position. Then return to the indicated position when you are ready.

Practice all of these etudes at a metronome marking between 80–132 beats per minute and experiment with a variety of different dynamics.

Third Position

Blues in C #1

Track 8

Third Position

Blues in C #2

Track 9

Third Position

Blues in C #3

Track 10

Fifth Position

Blues in B♭ #1 — Track 11

Fifth Position

Blues in B♭ #2 — Track 12

Fifth Position

Blues in B♭ #3 — Track 13

Fifth Position

Blues in D #1 Track 17

Fifth Position

Blues in D #2 Track 18

Fifth Position

Blues in D #3 Track 19

About Jazz Rhythms

At first, jazz rhythms may be confusing. There seems to be no end to the possible combinations of quarter notes, eighth notes, dotted notes and tied notes. This is true, but in jazz—as in any style—there are particular rhythmic phrases that are used over and over. Familiarizing yourself with the most common phrases will make reading much easier.

One very common rhythm is a dotted quarter followed by an eighth note:

The same rhythm could start on the second beat of a measure:

Or the third beat:

Notice that when the phrase starts on the second beat, it is written differently. Instead of using a dotted quarter, we use a tie from the second beat to the third beat. This makes reading easier by clearly showing how the measure can be broken into two smaller pieces:

It is also common to see our first phrase reversed:

And, again, you may see this same phrase starting on the second beat:

Or the third beat:

Another rhythm used frequently in jazz is the eighth-quarter-eighth.

It looks like this:

Here is a common variation on the above rhythm:

Remember, the point of studying these examples is to familiarize yourself with the most common jazz rhythms. Just as when learning to read the English language in school, you first had to learn the sound of each letter of the alphabet, then you learned simple words, like "cat" and "go." Eventually you progressed to harder words, then sentences, paragraphs, etc. Now you don't have to sound out each word. You can look at a sentence and grasp its meaning as a whole. Our goal in sight-reading is much the same. If you can look at a piece of music and recognize familiar patterns, you won't have to sound out each and every rhythm ("one, two-AND, three...") and will be able to read complex rhythmic phrases with ease.

Now let's look at two consecutive eighth notes. The following is a series of one-measure phrases using two eighth notes starting on each possible beat. Repeat each measure as many times as you like, then move on to the next measure. When you are comfortable with all of the rhythms, try playing the measures in reverse order or skipping around from measure to measure.

Section #2: Rhythm Studies

This section is made up of twelve rhythm studies. You should play these in as many positions as you can. Don't forget to use your metronome to help keep a steady groove.

Rhythm Study #1  Track 26

This study starts with a simple two-measure phrase using the first rhythm found on page 12. The phrase is repeated several times, adding one new measure each time.

Rhythm Study #2 Track 27

This one contains most of the tricky rhythms you're likely to encounter in ¾ time. Try clapping the rhythms a few times before reading it with your guitar.

Rhythm Study #3 Track 28

This study shows just how much you can do with one rhythm, in this case the dotted quarter.

♩ = 70-132

Rhythm Study #4 Track 29

Composed of three five-measure phrases, this study seems to turn the beat around.

♩ = 80-124

Rhythm Study #5  Track 30

This one contains many simple variations on its two-measure theme. The melody was inspired by the style of the great jazz guitarist Charlie Christian.

Rhythm Study #6 Track 31

Rhythm Study #7 Track 32

Here the challenge is quarter-note triplets. There are also a couple of half-note triplets.

Rhythm Study #8 Track 33

Again, the challenge here is triplets, but this study has more rests than Rhythm Study #7.

Rhythm Study #9  Track 34

Here again we see a theme (the first two measures) followed by variations (measures 3 and 4, and 5 and 6). Make sure you understand the rhythmic variations and are really reading, not just guessing

Rhythm Study #10 Track 35

This study is also theme and variations. The very first phrase (C-B-C) is the basis for the whole piece.

Rhythm Study #11  Track 36

This study starts with a six-note phrase and then moves it around. See how it repeats throughout the first eight measures? It's trickier than it looks.

Rhythm Study #12 Track 37

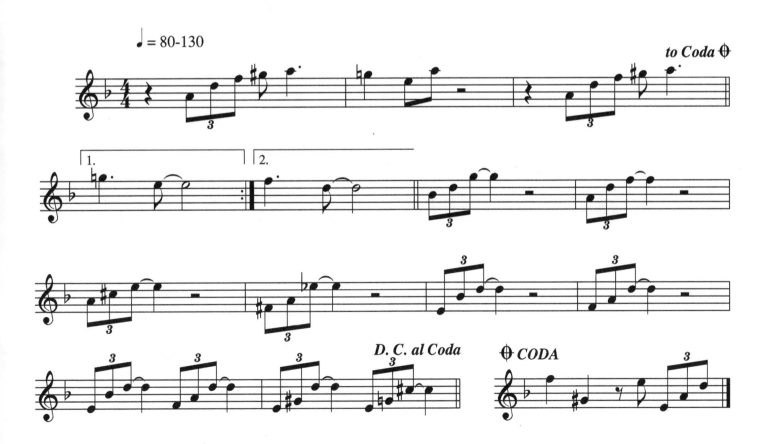

Section #3: Etudes Based on Jazz Standards

The etudes in this section are in the style of jazz standards that you are probably familiar with, such as *All the Things You Are* and *Stella by Starlight*. They can be played in any position. In fact, you should play each of them in several different positions. You can play these pieces at any tempo you like, but don't forget to swing!

St. Sonny  TRACK 38

Jonesing

22

Miles Standoffish

Track 40

(In the style of "All Blues")

With a blues feel ♩ = 102-120

Rhythm

Track 41

(In the style of "I Got Rhythm")

Bright jazz feel ♩ = 120-168

mf

to Coda ⊕

1.   2.

D. C. al Coda ⊕   ⊕ *CODA*

Waiting for Prince

Track 42

Jazz waltz ♩ = 102-132

(In the style of "Someday My Prince Will Come")

Harlem Express

Track 43

Bright swing feel ♩ = 140-168

(In the style of "Take the A Train")

26

Nowheresville Track 44

(In the style of "Out of Nowhere")

Like the Sun

 Track 45

Brightly ♩ = 132-160   (In the style of "Solar")

Stella  Track 46

(In the style of "Stella by Starlight")

Medium swing ♩ = 112-132

Althea

Medium swing ♩ = 112-132

(In the style of "All the Things You Are")

A11

Track 48

Medium swing ♩ = 112-132

(In the style of "All of Me")

Indiana Ticket

Track 49

Medium swing ♩ = 112-132

(In the style of "Donna Lee")

Section #4: Duets

This is the final section of the book, and we have saved the best for last. These pieces are duets, most of which are in the style of well-known jazz tunes. You should have fun playing these with a friend, teacher or the CD that is available.

Switch parts with your reading partner so that you each get to play both parts. If you are using the CD, you can isolate the parts using the balance control on your stereo.

Duet

Looking Glass TRACK 50

(In the style of "Alice in Wonderland")

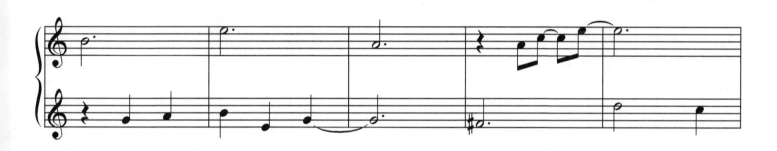

D. C. al Coda ⊕

⊕ CODA

Duet

When the Saints Go Marching In

Traditional

Brightly

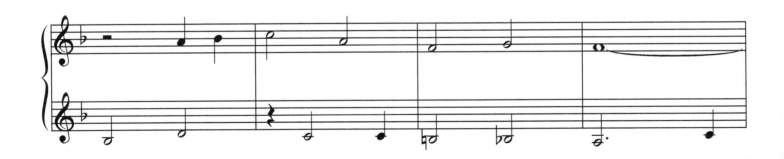

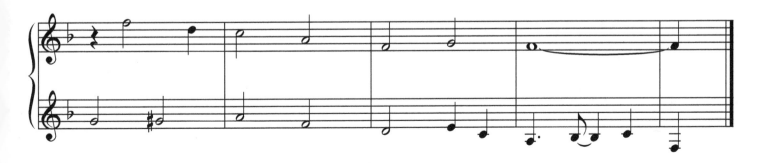

Duet

Fall

 Track 52

(In the style of "Autumn Leaves")

Moderately

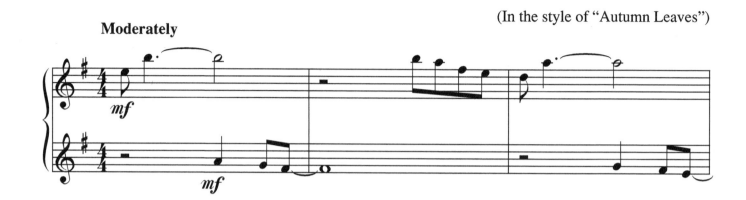

Duet

Dolphins on Green Street

 Track 53

(In the style of "On Green Dolphin Street")

Moderate Bossa Nova

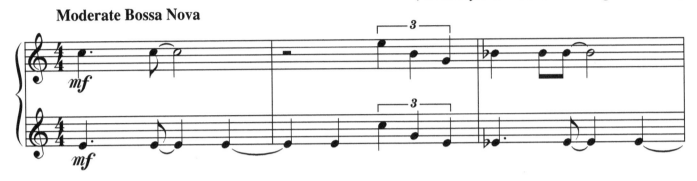

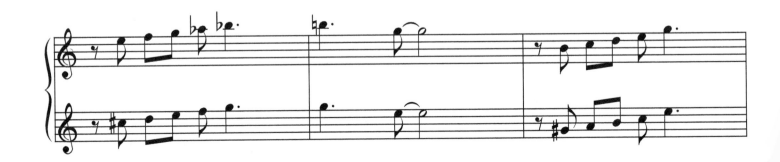

D. C. al Coda ⊕   ⊕ *CODA*

harm.

40

Duet

Hymn-like

Track 54

Slowly

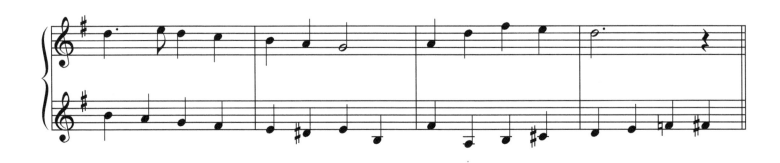

41

Duet **Three Phases**  Track 55

Moderately, with a Blues feeling

Duet

Boppin' Etude Track 56

(In the style of "Scrapple from the Apple")

Brightly

to Coda ⊕

D. C. al Coda ⊕

⊕ *CODA*

Duet

Georgia Brown Suite

 Track 57

(In the style of "Sweet Georgia Brown")

Brightly

to Coda ⊕

D. C. al Coda ⊕   ⊕ *CODA*

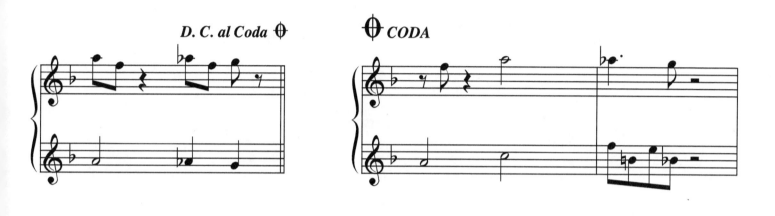

46

Duet

Kenny D.  Track 58

(In the style of "Blue Bossa")

Bossa Nova feel

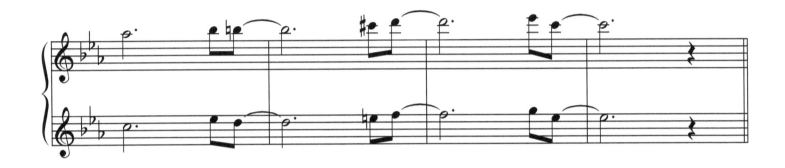

Duet

Adios, Amigo Track 59

(In the style of "Bye Bye Blackbird")

What's Next?

Now that you've completed this book, what's next? In order to keep your sight-reading chops in top form, sight-reading must become part of your regular daily practice. You should get your hands on as much music as possible and read, read, read. A book of Charlie Parker solos, a book of Miles Davis solos...you might even want to try some classical music such as Bach or Mozart. Anything that will help you develop as a player and as a reader is good, and being a good reader will open up the entire musical world to you. You might even want a book on music theory such as *Teach Yourself Guitar Theory* or *Theory for the Contemporary Guitarist*. So, don't put your music stand back in the closet just yet. Keep reading, and keep swinging!